D0787342

2⁰⁰
H

Pippa Funnell

Follow Your Dreams

Orion
Children's Books

Factfile

"I'm a great believer that however serious things get you've got to have some fun and have a laugh."

BIRTHPLACE
Crowborough, East Sussex, England

FULL NAME
Philippa Rachel Funnell

LIVES IN
Dorking, Surrey

OLD SURNAME
Nolan

BIRTHDAY
7th October

STAR SIGN
Libra

BEEN RIDING SINCE
About four years old

CHINESE STAR SIGN
Monkey

MARRIED
Yes, to international show jumper, William Funnell

FEARS AND PHOBIAS
The dentist, needles and injections

FAVOURITE HOBBY
Skiing

OTHER SPORTS
Lacrosse at school and tennis

FAVOURITE FOOD
Lamb chops, mashed potatoes and broccoli

FAVOURITE PETS
Dogs, especially terriers

HAIR COLOUR
Chestnut brown

EYE COLOUR
Blue

FAVOURITE PLACE TO CHILL
In the garden

BEAUTY SECRET
Lots of moisturiser, essential when you're outside a lot, like Pippa

FITNESS SECRET
Riding every day and working hard in the yard

THREE-DAY EVENTING HEROES
Lucinda Green, Ginny Leng and Mark Todd

OTHER SPORTING HEROES
Steve Redgrave and Paula Radcliffe

"A lot of people think that a horse is just an animal that requires feeding and looking after, but to me most of them are people; they know who you are, and they react to you."

"An inspiration to those who aspire"
Horse and Hound

5

Meet Pippa

Pippa's story is an inspirational tale for anyone who has a dream. It all began when she was a little girl, learning to ride on a borrowed horse and building jumps in the back garden with her friends. It was a long way from the excitement and glamour of Badminton and Burghley, but Pippa's passion, ambition and hard work have taken her all the way to the biggest and best eventing competitions in the world.

It was Pippa's mum, Jenny, who first encouraged her to ride. Jenny had ridden since her teens and worked full-time organising equestrian events. She used to take Pippa to watch the Horse of the Year show every October as a birthday treat. Pippa began riding and competing when she was just six, and won her first gymkhana too.

By the time she was fourteen and had her first horse, Sir Barnaby, Pippa's dream of becoming a champion eventer was starting to take shape.

"...what has happened to me has made me realise that anything is possible in life, if only you can somehow hold on to your dream..."

Pippa insists she isn't naturally talented but that she has really had to work at it. She has fallen off her horses more than a few times on the way to the top, but she's always got straight back on.

And though she achieved more than she ever thought possible when she became the world's Number One, winning the Rolex Grand Slam in 2003 – wow! – she's just as down-to-earth and hardworking as ever.

PIPPA THE STORYTELLER

Busy Pippa manages to find time to write a series of children's books, *Tilly's Pony Tails*. When Tilly helps rescue neglected horse, Magic Spirit, she's invited to Silver Shoe Farm to help with his recovery and discovers she has a very special gift.

With her boundless enthusiasm and winning ways with horses, Tilly bears more than a passing resemblance to Pippa. It's important to Pippa that her readers realise you don't have to be able to afford a horse or pony – there are other ways to ride if you're really determined. In the stories, Tilly wears a woven bracelet made from horsehair – and there's a story behind that too:

"I had the most wonderful horse called Viceroy who was sadly lost through colic," Pippa recalls. "His owners sent part of his tail off to America to be made into bracelets and while driving I noticed mine and had the idea for the story."

ANIMAL LOVER

It goes without saying that Pippa adores her horses. They work just as hard as she does and in return they are cared for, loved and rewarded.

> *"Even as a small child, I had a strong relationship with my ponies; they weren't just tools for winning rosettes, I loved being with them. They were my special friends."*

Pippa also has a special place in her heart for her dogs – and she's always filled her home with them. Her first dog was Fingers, a scruffy Jack Russell puppy. She's since had Spliff, a feisty Lakeland cross terrier who loved hunting; and Toes, a pretty tan terrier who drove her decorators mad by running off with their paintbrushes and walking through paint trays. Then came Fudge, a black-and-tan terrier puppy, known to all as 'Fudgey Funnell'.

And also two little terrier sisters, Mouse and Zippy – Pippa gave them both a home because she couldn't bear to part them. Mouse had puppies, of which Pippa kept two, Tom and Weasel.

WORLD HORSE WELFARE

There's no doubt Pippa's got a big heart. But she doesn't just care for her own horses – she cares about *all* horses. She's a trustee of the charity, World Horse Welfare. WHW is dedicated to giving abused and neglected horses a second chance in life by rescuing and re-homing them. In the UK, WHW have four farms open to visitors where many of their 2,000 horses are kept. For more information go to: www.worldhorsewelfare.org

FUNNELL FACTOR

Look out for the Funnell Factor tour. In this evening of horsey fun, Pippa and William entertain audiences by riding some of their top horses from the world of show jumping and eventing, including their own Billy Stud homebred horses.

The show combines serious training and nutritional advice with hilarious riding stunts as Pippa and William give each other light-hearted lessons in their own areas of expertise. They first took to the road in 2004 and it was such a success that they toured again in 2010. It always means lots of driving and late nights for the couple, but it's a great chance for them to meet and talk to their fans and they enjoy putting on the shows, especially when they're making fun of each other!

LIBRA

Pippa is a typically well-balanced Libran. She has ambition and determination but this doesn't stop her from chilling with friends and letting her hair down. Librans have the gift of understanding the emotional needs of their companions, which is how she forms such special relationships with her horses.

PIPPA IN 3D!

Pippa has also put her famous face and name to a range of Ubisoft computer games, in which you can train, groom and care for horses, run stables and enter competitions. In some of the games, you can even meet Pippa as a 3D character!

Big Dreams

Aged six, Pippa was given a pony called Pepsi by one of her mum's friends and she began learning to ride and entering gymkhanas. No one could have guessed then how successful she was going to be. But as she and her friend Ally played on their ponies in the paddock, Pippa imagined she was a famous rider competing at the Badminton Horse Trials. And as she lay in bed at night, she dreamed of winning a medal at the Olympic Games.

Pippa wasn't just a daydreamer though – she knew what she wanted and she made it happen! When she was seven she joined her local Pony Club. The Pony Club was the perfect place for Pippa to learn more about riding and caring for horses. Pippa is full of praise for the Pony Club.

Pippa lived for her riding lessons and took the Pony Club rallies very seriously, keeping a detailed diary of all her results at the gymkhanas.

Saturday
Jeremy Fisher jumped well today, but got a bit upset in thunderstorm.

"I was a member of the Eridge Branch and my mother still helps with the organising of various competitions. You can only get out what you put in. Do not be afraid to ask for advice from those more experienced than yourself – we all need advice and never stop learning!"

PIPPA'S PONIES

♥ PEPSI ♥

A long way from the top-class horses Pippa rides today, her first pony was a funny little thing, small, black and hairy, about 11.2 hh, who lived in a field and was always really muddy in the winter.

♥ FLIGHTY ♥

Pippa was nine when Ruth McMullen, legendary riding teacher and a friend of Pippa's mum's, found Flighty for her. He was a young pony, not quite four years old, and only just broken. Pippa was quick to learn that caring for your pony isn't all about spending lots of money and having fantastic facilities – it's about time, love and good horse management.

♥ JEREMY FISHER ♥

At eleven, Pippa grew out of Flighty, and Ruth McMullen found her Jeremy Fisher. He was 13.2 hh and a bit of a handful. Pippa found her ability to get on with ponies was really put to the test!

Pippa loved her ponies – even the tricky ones – and there were a lot of tears when she finally had to move onto a horse.

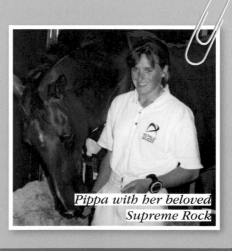

Pippa with her beloved Supreme Rock

In the Spotlight

"Dreams can come true, but boy, do you need to put a huge amount of work in and have plenty of patience, dedication and determination and a whole heap of luck. It's a very long staircase but worth climbing up."

1986 **Team bronze**: Junior European Championships (Airborne)

1987 **Individual gold**: Young Rider European Championships (Sir Barnaby)

1988 **8th and team gold**: Young Rider European Championships (Sir Barnaby)

1989 **Individual silver and team silver**: Young Rider European Championships (Sir Barnaby)

1999 **Individual gold and team gold**: European Championships (Supreme Rock)

2000 **Team silver**: Sydney Olympic Games (Supreme Rock)

2001 **Individual gold and team gold**: European Championships (Supreme Rock)

2002 **Team bronze**: World Equestrian Games (Supreme Rock)

2003 **Team gold and individual bronze**: European Championships (Walk On Star)

2003 **Grand Slam**: Badminton, Kentucky and Burghley (Supreme Rock and Primmore's Pride)

2004 **Team silver and individual bronze**: Athens Olympic Games (Primmore's Pride)

2005 **1st**: Badminton (Primmore's Pride)

2010 **1st**: Bramham (Redesigned)

TITLES, TROPHIES AND TV

1992

Horse and Hound Personality of the Year voted for by the readers

Pippa appeared on A Question of Sport on rugby player Bill Beaumont's team. She got all the eventing questions right, *"but I was absolutely clueless about everything else."*

Winner of the British Equestrian Writers Association trophy, voted for by journalists and presented at the Olympia Horse Show. Pippa loves the Christmassy atmosphere of Olympia, and the ending of one of her books, *Samson the Stallion*, is set there.

Also presented at Olympia was a new trophy, the Raymond Brooks-Ward Memorial Trophy, for the most promising under-25 rider in show jumping, dressage and eventing. Pippa struggled to hold back the tears when she received the award. Raymond Brooks-Ward had been her godfather, and it was he and his wife who had lent Pepsi to Pippa all those years ago.

2003

Sportswoman of the Year by *The Sunday Times*. Equestrian of the Year
BBC South Sports Personality of the Year
The Pat Besford Award for the Outstanding Sporting Achievement of the Year

2004

Invited to a 'Women of Achievement' lunch with the Queen at Buckingham Palace, Pippa was thrilled when the comedian Jennifer Saunders recognised her and came to say hello.

2005

Invited on to A Question of Sport again. Pippa was on a team with footballer Ally McCoist and athlete Jade Johnson – and they won!

Pippa was awarded an MBE in the Queen's Birthday Honours.
"I was overwhelmingly thrilled: what an honour!"

"I still find these big sporting occasions extraordinary and don't feel worthy of being in such a line-up."

Eventing

Growing up, Pippa idolised champion event riders, like Lucinda Green, Ginny Leng and Mark Todd. Aged fourteen, after reading Lucinda Green's autobiography, *Up, Up and Away*, she knew she wanted to focus on eventing. Pippa quickly fell in love with the magic and atmosphere of the sport. And it was with her first horse, Sir Barnaby, that Pippa's plans began to take shape.

Eventing is the ultimate challenge for both horse and rider, as it doesn't just test one skill, it tests three very different skills – dressage, cross-country and show jumping. The tests take place over one, two or three days, but the competitor must ride the same horse throughout – so once you've chosen your horse, you have to stick with it, no matter what goes wrong. Pippa set herself a tough task, but as her record-breaking results have proved, she made the perfect choice.

Harmony with your horse is so important in eventing, and Pippa's talent for understanding her horses would lead her to success.

"One of the special things about our sport is that, with young horses being brought on all the time, even at grass-roots level you can compete against the top people – there are probably young people who get a serious buzz from beating me now, and it gives them incentive and hope."

DRESSAGE

TOP 6 SKILLS

🐎 PRECISION

🐎 PATIENCE

🐎 HARMONY

🐎 BALANCE

🐎 RHYTHM

🐎 CO-ORDINATION

The first challenge is the dressage test. The horse performs a variety of movements in straight lines and circles, using letters around the arena as a guide. Not every horse enjoys doing these controlled movements or keeping within an enclosed area, but an eventing horse has to be an all-rounder. Pippa works endlessly with her horses to achieve perfection. If they are performing well, the horse looks as though he is doing all the movements on his own – but of course, Pippa is communicating with her horse all the time, and it's a real test of the bond between them.

"One of the most important lessons Barnaby taught me is that the worst thing a rider can do is nothing, sitting frozen by fear that the horse will explode. No matter what a horse does underneath you, when you're doing a dressage test you've got to get on and ride them."

CROSS-COUNTRY

- 🐎 **TRUST**
- 🐎 **SPEED**
- 🐎 **BRAVERY**
- 🐎 **ENDURANCE**
- 🐎 **ATHLETICISM**
- 🐎 **TIMING AND PACE**

TOP 6 SKILLS

Cross-country is next. It tests the speed, endurance and jumping ability of the horse. Both horse and rider have to be physically fit and fearless, so it isn't a sport for the faint-hearted! A cross-country course is designed to be difficult – with breath-taking water features like ponds and streams, together with different jumps, drops and ditches. Pippa, like the other riders, always walks the course before the competition, and plans out how best to tackle each obstacle. But for the horse, it will be new territory, and even the best-laid plans don't always work out.

"…it is that ability to cope with the inevitable glitches in a cross-country round and quickness in retrieving the situation that marks out the class cross-country riders…"

SHOW JUMPING

TOP 6
SKILLS

🐎 **NERVE**

🐎 **CARE**

🐎 **FITNESS**

🐎 **OBEDIENCE**

🐎 **ATHLETICISM**

🐎 **SUPPLENESS OF HORSE**

The grand finale is the show jumping test, held in an arena in front of a large audience. Horse and rider face a series of between twelve and fourteen brightly-coloured fences – that can be knocked down, and at top level measuring 1.3 metres. Penalties are given for any obstacle knocked down, as well as any second over the time limit, so tensions run high. You can just imagine the sense of anticipation on the final day of an event, the exhilaration of a clear round or the heartbreak as the fences fall!

A Sense of Style

Fashion isn't one of Pippa's top priorities – her horses come first – but she certainly has her own sense of style. Of course, it helps that she's pretty and petite, with naturally shiny long chestnut hair. She looks good whatever she wears!

TEAM TOGGI

Pippa was involved in designing a new range of breeches for Toggi, which were a great success. Toggi also became the official clothing sponsors to the British equestrian team.

Pippa has been sponsored by Toggi for nearly fifteen years and loves their clothes.

FAVOURITE TOGGI PRODUCT AND WHY?

"I couldn't choose – I use a whole range of Toggi products and everything is great, but I particularly love the breeches."

FASHION FUN

Pippa had to laugh when all of her winning riding clothes from Badminton, which she'd left in a bin bag for washing, were carted away by the dustbin men!

MOST TREASURED ACCESSORY

Rolex watch – Pippa was awarded the watch for winning the Grand Slam, and she became an ambassador for Rolex.

BIG BLACK BOOTS

Like every young rider, Pippa couldn't wait to get a pair of long boots. But the very first time she proudly wore them, she caught one of the boots on a nail sticking out of a post, which ripped it to shreds. The boots were ruined, but if she hadn't been wearing them, her leg would have been a horrible mess!

FASHION SHOOT

Pippa is often photographed in action, but it was something out of the ordinary when *The Sunday Times* invited her and fellow team-mates to a glamorous fashion shoot. It was a day to remember, and she loved "the most fantastic pale blue silk dress" she was given to wear.

The Road to Success

When Pippa was fourteen, she said a tearful goodbye to her last pony, Jeremy Fisher, and hello to Sir Barnaby, her first horse – chosen for her by trainer, Ruth McMullen. Little did Pippa know that Sir Barnaby was to take her further than she'd ever dreamed possible.

Two years later, when Pippa was offered the opportunity to train as a working pupil in Norfolk with Ruth, she jumped at the chance. Living in, she would ride anything up to nine or ten horses a day – the best possible grounding for a rider – as well as having the benefit of lessons from Ruth.

Rising at 7am and working twelve-hour days was exhausting, and the mucking-out was back-breaking, but Pippa didn't let anything put her off. She quickly proved herself through hard work and a determined attitude. Watching Ruth's calm but firm handling of the horses inspired Pippa to achieve the same harmony with her own horses.

> *"I find it fascinating how each horse is so different and love trying to work out how each one thinks"*

At first, Pippa wasn't sure Sir Barnaby was cut out for dressage, though he was brilliant at cross-country and show jumping. But with Ruth's expert tuition, they turned him into a champion. In 1987, Pippa and Sir Barnaby won the individual gold together at the Young Rider European Championships, making Pippa the under-21 champion of Europe. They were thrust into the spotlight and finally ready for their first Badminton.

SIR BARNABY – BAD BOY!

Mischievous Barnaby used to get very cross if Pippa forgot to give him a peppermint, and sometimes he'd let people lead him to his stable and then reverse back to his field. Even as an older horse, he could still be naughty. Embarrassingly at the indoor shows at prize-givings, he would drag Pippa into the ring when he heard the music – even when they hadn't won!

WHAT A NICE LITTLE HORSE!

Imagine Pippa's delight at the British Novice Championships when her heroine, eventing champion Lucinda Green, came up to her and said that Sir Barnaby was "a nice little horse". Now Pippa always tries to make the effort to talk to younger riders, because Lucinda's words meant so much to her.

PIPPA'S CHOSEN PATH

Like most anxious parents, Pippa's were worried that a career in horses might not work out, and wanted to make sure she had other skills. To keep them happy, she did a secretarial course in London, and worked four nights a week as a waitress in a local restaurant. But Pippa knew exactly what she wanted to do – and it wasn't secretarial work!

"I was absolutely convinced that I wanted a life with horses."

RUTH MCMULLEN: TRAINER, MENTOR AND FRIEND

"Ruth is a perfectionist and so am I. Several times I remember being quite pleased with my performance in a competition, and she would point out where I had gone wrong and what I could have done better. I might have felt a bit flat for a few days, but looking back, I see that was what set my standards so high. Looking at the video of my performances in the Olympics, I don't think: 'Great, I got a medal.' I analyse what I could do better. I only enter competitions I think myself, and the horse, are ready for, and an awful lot of that attitude is due to Ruth."

Pippa's Pals

LIZZIE BUNN

Occupation: Equestrian event organiser, particularly of Hickstead

Special connection: Lizzie chose Pippa to be her daughter Georgia's godmother

Fun times together: Pippa and William fell in love with skiing on their first holiday in the Alps with Lizzie

"We must have fallen over forty times, and by the end we were crying with laughter."

TINA COOK

Occupation: Athlete (eventing)

Star sign: Virgo

First friends: 1989, when they were both in the squad for the championships in Achselshwang, Bavaria

Special talent: Cross-country riding

Fun times together: Pippa and Tina love travelling to events together

"Tina and I never run out of things to talk about and can always fill the journey, no matter what the length, with continuous chat. Tina's a good person to come home from an event with, win or lose."

WILLIAM FOX-PITT

Occupation: Professional Event Rider and Trainer

Star sign: Capricorn

First friends: During Pippa's Pony Club days

Married to: Alice Plunkett, a talented and successful racing TV presenter – "one of the nicest, kindest, funniest people"

Friendly rivals: People talk about the rivalry between William and Pippa *"but really there isn't any"*

CHRIS WARREN AND DUNCAN GIPSON

Occupation: Equine dentist
Fun Fact: Chris was an usher at Pippa and William's wedding
Good times together: *"Many holidays, all of which have been highly entertaining. With them I behave like a kid, always finding pranks and tricks to play."*

ANTOINETTE MCKEOWEN

Occupation: Event rider
Star sign: Gemini
Good times together: *"Tina, Ants and I are all great mates, both of us are godmothers to Tina's kids. Ants introduced us to Botswana. We have been on safari there twice with her, which gave me an idea for one of my books."*

TEAM PIPPA

NINI FRENCH

When Nini came to Pippa as head girl it was to be a temporary arrangement – but she ended up staying for five years, and going with Pippa to the Olympics!

"She did a fantastic job at turning the horses out, she rode beautifully and she was a good friend who had become part of my life. But her aim was always to compete herself and have a yard. I was very sad when she left."

ZANIE TANSWELL

Zanie came as head girl when Nini French left, and she and Pippa soon bonded. Zanie loved working with Pippa but eventually decided to move in with her boyfriend, Chris King, who had a yard of his own.

HANNAH BAILEY

Followed Zanie as head girl. She was with Pippa for five years. She carried on with the extremely high standards. She left at the end of 2009. She struck up an incredibly special bond with Ensign so Pippa gave him to her. Abby Farmer has now taken over as head girl.

Wedding Bells

Pippa and William Funnell are one of the best-known couples in the horse riding world. William is an international show jumper and a top horse breeder. Together they live on a beautiful farm in the Surrey countryside. And of course it goes without saying that their home includes a large number of stables!

When Pippa first knew William, she was still at school – he'd already left and seemed very grown-up. She's since confessed that she used to go home and dream about him! In her early twenties they met again at shows, and as they moved in the same horse riding circles, William and Pippa soon got to know each other and became friends – but there was already some chemistry between them.

> "I found myself thinking about him a lot, not in a totally besotted way but certainly with a buzz of excitement."

Pippa fell in love with William's wonderful sense of humour, and the fact that he's always been able to bring her back down to earth. She respects his riding abilities and his good relationships with his horses – something that's very important to Pippa.

Romance blossomed. It wasn't easy, with William living in Surrey and Pippa still at Ruth's in Norfolk, but they were determined to make it work.

After nearly two years together, when Pippa was driving to visit William, she made a wish that he would propose – and that very night he popped the question!

The ceremony was held in Tidebrook village church where Pippa had sung in the choir during her schooldays, and the reception was at Possingworth Manor in Uckfield, for all their family and friends. Pippa had a hen night in Lizzie Bunn's local pub – and her friends got her a gorilla-gram! For the wedding, Pippa wore her mum's beautiful dress, bringing tears to her dad's eyes.

The Will to Win

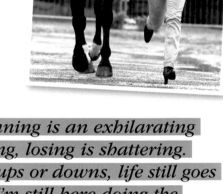

Thanks to a combination of determination and dedication, Pippa has made her dreams a reality. From her first event, aged sixteen, it took nineteen years for Pippa to achieve her World Number One status, but she never gave up.

In the early days at Ruth McMullen's school, the long hours would have put many girls off for life.

"Winning is an exhilarating feeling, losing is shattering. But ups or downs, life still goes on, I'm still here doing the washing."

"I was in tears after every lesson for the first few weeks at Ruth's. She would not let me out of a walk. She said unless I got the walk correct, I had no chance in trot. Her attention to detail is staggering."

Today, Pippa is still out early, working around the stables, schooling up to ten horses in the day. She now struggles to find time for teaching.

Even after a big win and the flurry of presentations, press conferences, photo-calls and celebrations – it's back down to earth for Pippa, packing everything back up and driving the lorry home, triumphant but exhausted!

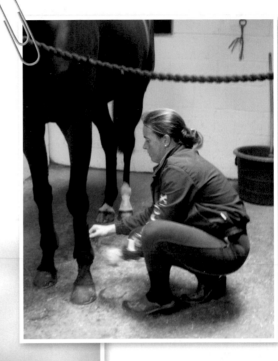

"Winning is amazing for a minute, but then I am striving again to reach my next goals."

A Supreme Champion

"Rocky is the most amazing horse on whom to ride a test when there's a lot of atmosphere. He just rises to the occasion … this in turn makes my spirits rise and I feel proud and exhilarated – it makes me want to show him off as best as I can."

Achieving at the major events takes a special rider, but also a special horse. With Supreme Rock, one of Pippa's most famous horses, (affectionately known as Rocky), Pippa won individual gold and team gold at the European Championships – not once, but twice! At the Sydney Olympic Games, Pippa rode Rocky when Team GB won the silver medal. When Pippa won the Grand Slam in 2003, it was with Rocky, as well as one of her other star horses, Primmore's Pride. Rocky is also one of a select group of horses who have won the Badminton Horse Trials twice, in 2002 and 2003.

SUPREME ROCK

🐎 Irish Thoroughbred
🐎 Bay
🐎 16.3 hh

"I'd known since 1999 that I was capable of winning Badminton on Rocky, but it seemed such a long time coming."

Grand Slam

In 2003, Pippa made history. She became the first (and only!) person to win eventing's most coveted prize – the Rolex Grand Slam. Winning three of the big events in a row – Kentucky, Badminton and Burghley – the Grand Slam is considered the toughest three-day eventing slam in the sporting world.

"It hasn't turned me into a different person. The feeling of winning lasts only a split second compared to the lifetime of striving for that moment."

The Badminton cross-country course is designed to be the most intimidating challenge for a horse and rider, so no one ever imagined that when the event first started, a mere woman would be charging around this course, competing against the men on equal terms.

Even after her sucess at Kentucky and Badminton, Pippa never imagined she was in line for the Grand Slam. After all, she still had to conquer Burghley.

At Burghley, the atmosphere was electric. Pippa and her horse, Primmore's Pride (Kiri) performed as though their lives depended on it – and triumphed!

"Kiri's show jumping round that day was one of the best I have ever ridden at a three-day event. He was simply fantastic."

Pippa had achieved more than she'd ever dreamed possible – the Grand Slam was hers!

Pippa won the Rolex watch – her most prized possession – and joked that at last she could throw away the plastic Swatch that her brother Tim had given her one Christmas.

From the little girl who'd ridden Pepsi, the muddy pony given to her by a friend, Pippa was now the Number One Ranked Rider in the World. And in true Pippa style, when the thrill of winning had passed and the celebrations were over, she was straight back to work.

"When I said in the Burghley press conference that winning $250,000 wasn't going to change the fact that I still had to wash up on Monday morning, I wasn't joking. I still had loads of boring jobs to do. It was a very long drive back to Forest Green from Lincolnshire, and I had just twenty-four hours to gallop three horses and get organised for two weeks away at Blenheim and the European Championships in Punchestown, Ireland."

Superstars

BITS AND PIECES

(owned by Sarah and Richard Jewson)

Pippa never imagined Bits and Pieces (nicknamed Henry) might be a horse for the big time when she first saw him at Ruth's. He was a good jumper but tricky in the dressage.

"Still there was something special about this little horse. He was like a tiger across country, so hungry to jump the fences."

By this time, Pippa and William lived at Cobbetts Farm, and Pippa agreed to stable Henry for his owners on a trial basis. She came to believe that Henry could be a top-level prospect. Together they competed at Blenheim in 1995, and Pippa's belief in Henry paid off – they won first prize!

*Bits and Pieces
(Nickname: Henry)
Skewbald Gelding
15.3 hh*

PRIMMORE'S PRIDE

(owned by Roger and Denise Lincoln)

Primmore's Pride oozed star potential from the beginning. A bold athletic horse, with a wonderful temperament for dressage, Pippa was impressed by his spectacular feel across country and superb jump.

"I knew I was sitting on one of the best horses in the world."

Primmore's Pride has already made history by winning three traditional four-star three-day events: Kentucky and Burghley in 2003, and Badminton in 2005.

And he has another claim to fame – one of Pippa's books, *Pride and Joy the event horse,* is dedicated to him.

"He is big, bold, and beautifully balanced and, at 11-years old, approaching his prime. He is subtle enough to handle the equine ballet of the dressage, tough enough to endure the daunting jumps and 10 unforgiving minutes of the cross-country. But he depends on Pippa – and she on him."
The Telegraph

*Primmore's Pride
(Nickname: Kiri)
Bay 7/8 Thoroughbred
15.3 hh*

Pippa adores all her horses. She works hard with every one of them so that they each have the opportunity to shine. And some of them have shone very brightly indeed.

ENSIGN

(owned by Pippa and her mother, Jenny Nolan)

An ex-racehorse, Ensign had to be entirely retrained for eventing. That's even more work than starting from scratch with a young horse. But Pippa was very excited about Ensign's potential – she and her mum had bought him as an investment.

Ensign narrowly lost an individual medal at the 2005 European Championships, but he and Pippa trained hard to win second place at Pau in late 2007, which put them on the shortlist for the 2008 Olympics.

Ensign
(Nickname: Titch)
Bay Thoroughbred
16 hh

WALK ON STAR

(owned by Nick and Barbara Walkinshaw)

Walk on Star
(Nickname: Magic)
Bay 7/8 Thorough-
bred 16.2 hh

Pippa is full of praise for this kind-natured and clever horse, whose level-headed attitude to competitions is exactly what's needed at big events.

"Walk on Star (Magic) changed from a boy to a man last year winning at Saumur, and then being part of the gold medal team and winning an individual bronze at the European Eventing Championships at Punchestown. This was a real thrill as deep down I felt that if he went well he might be lucky and get into the top ten. Again he showed us how he comes up with the goods when it matters."

Sydney Olympics 2000

Every sportsman or woman's wildest dream is to be chosen to represent their country at the greatest sporting event in the world – the Olympics. So when Pippa was chosen for Team GB at the Sydney Olympics, she was delighted, and got straight to work preparing herself and Supreme Rock for the challenge.

"Getting into the team was a huge honour and achievement."

In the dressage, all of Team GB had personal bests, and Pippa and Rocky were in second place – a brilliant start! Next came the cross-country, and though Pippa was feeling nervous, she had a fantastic ride. With only the show jumping to go, Team GB were in second place behind the Australian team, and hopes were high for a medal. In the end, Team GB narrowly missed the gold, but were worthy winners of the silver. A brilliant result for Team GB – and for Pippa!

"I knew that the more hopes I pinned on it, the greater the possibility of disappointment."

"When I stepped into that Olympic stadium, I could hardly convince myself I was really there. The whole experience was like a dream: but deep down, I knew I had to keep my head and stay focused."

TEAM GB

JEANETTE BRAKEWELL ON OVER TO YOU

A brilliant cross-country rider, and the winner of three successive team golds at the European Championship.

IAN STARK ON JAYBEE

The oldest of the team, at aged forty-five, this was Ian's fifth Olympics.

PIPPA FUNNELL ON SUPREME ROCK

Pippa loved being part of the whole team spirit – it was a very special feeling.

LESLIE LAW ON SHEAR H2O

This was Leslie's first Olympics as a member of Team GB. He rode a Grey Irish Sport Horse on the cross-country course.

A SILVER MEDAL

"All of us were overwhelmed with the pride we felt in being part of Team GB"

It was a proud moment when Team GB stood on the podium and waved to the crowd. They could see all the British people in the audience waving back with their Union Jacks.

"It sank in that we'd flown these horses to the other side of the world, we hadn't let our country down – we hadn't actually let anyone down – and we were bringing home an Olympic medal."

Athens Olympics 2004

"The Olympics is such a big deal – literally the culmination of a lifetime's work."

Another Olympics and another call-up for Pippa! After her Grand Slam success in 2003, she was expecting to be selected, "but it was still a relief and a thrill to get the actual call."

The Athens Olympics posed a new challenge – the heat. Pippa started running or cycling every day to increase her fitness levels, and she galloped Primmore's Pride regularly in a special fleece rug to acclimatise the horse to the 90°c heat expected in Athens. As always, her horse's well-being was the priority.

"I know it's the Olympics and it's special, but we've still got to ride with our heads. If I feel my horse is tiring because of the heat I will slacken off. Our horses have to come first."

"EXPERIENCE OF A LIFETIME"

Pippa was one of the Olympic torch-bearers carrying the flame on its journey through London. She was the penultimate torch-bearer, lighting Sir Steve Redgrave's torch outside Buckingham Palace.

WILLIAM FOX–PITT ON TAMARILLO
William has lived and breathed horses all his life.

MARY KING ON KING SOLOMON III
Mary was reserve and replaced Sarah at the last minute. Mary wasn't from a horsey background, she'd done all sorts of jobs – gardener, cook, chalet girl – to fund her training.

JEANETTE BRAKEWELL ON OVER TO YOU
Pippa knew from previous experience that Jeanette would be crucial to team success, so was delighted to have her on board.

SARAH CUTTERIDGE ON THE WEXFORD LADY
Nicknamed 'Cool Cutty' by the rest of the team for her calm attitude at competitions. Sadly, The Wexford Lady went lame before the event and Sarah missed out on her Olympic dream.

TEAM GB

PIPPA FUNNELL ON PRIMMORE'S PRIDE
If people asked when Pippa began preparing Primmore's Pride for the Olympics, she'd reply, "Nine years ago – when he was only two!"

LESLIE LAW ON SHEAR L'EAU
As well as his contribution to team silver, Leslie won an individual gold.

Team GB performed brilliantly again and won another well deserved silver medal, with individual bronze for Pippa. It was an amazing result at the highest level of athletic achievement.

Redesigned: A New Champion

Pippa was out of the spotlight for a few years, but she couldn't stay away for long, and 2010 saw her back with a star in the making – a handsome chestnut called Redesigned.

In June 2010, Pippa won her third Bramham International Horse Trials title with Redesigned – and their stunning performance included a clear show jumping round in the pouring rain.

By the end of that year, Redesigned was ranked fifth in the British Eventing Top 100 Horses. What a fantastic comeback for Pippa with this exciting young horse! And he's already made his way into Pippa's *Tilly's Pony Tails* books, as a racehorse called Red Admiral.

"It's been a hard road to get to the top, I now know that staying there is even harder."

Champions
of the Future

Pippa's triumphant comeback with Redesigned certainly put her back in the spotlight, but she's also busy working with the champion horses of the future.

THE BILLY STUD

Pippa, her husband, William, and top breeder Donal Barnwell have been working together since 1997 to produce champion sports horses for the future. The combination of their experience in show jumping, eventing and breeding, is already proving a winning formula.

"It's just got bigger and bigger, and I've become increasingly involved," says Pippa. "Donal does the stud work; William and I, with the help of our dedicated team, do all the producing – from three years of age upwards. Our aim is to produce top-class sports horses for show jumping and eventing."

Pippa on Billy on Show

In 2009, Pippa was brimming with enthusiasm for two of their young horses. "I've just come back from the Burghley Horse Trials . . . two of my young horses took first and second places in the five-year-old Young Event Horse Final. Billy Be Cool won the class, and stable-mate Billy Beware took second place, so it was a double celebration."

In 2010, at the Four-Year-Old Young Event Horse Finals at Burghley, Pippa rode Billy Pastime and achieved fifth place, with Billy My Star just behind in sixth place. And Billy Bounce is yet another of the young horses in the Billy Stud programme to watch out for – in 2010 he made it to sixth in the British Eventing Top 100 Horses on Foundation Points with Chris King.

"I now know," says Pippa, *"that I do what I do not to win – though I am very competitive – but because I love the day to day working with horses."*

What's next for Pippa?

Following her dreams has taken Pippa all the way to the top. From the Grand Slam and her Number One ranking to Olympics medals; from the Pippa Funnell computer games to the *Tilly's Pony Tails* books and Pippa's own autobiography; from talented young horses emerging from the Billy Stud to the international stage.

One thing's for sure, Pippa isn't planning on stopping any time soon.

Watch this space!

STOP PRESS! ★☆★☆✦

ASK PIPPA

Pippa invited fans to send in all their horse and pony questions for a new book which published in 2011. Inside she reveals the answers to all the little things you've EVER wanted to know about horses. An essential read for horse and pony lovers everywhere.

THE BILLY STUD

The Billy Stud is thrilled to have no fewer than seven young horses on track for both show jumping and eventing at the 2012 London Olympics.

TILLY'S PONY TAILS

Pippa's series continues to grow in popularity – look out for more books in the pipeline!

OLYMPIC ASPIRATIONS

With the 2012 London Olympics on the horizon, Pippa could be a serious contender. "I would love to be at London if I had a horse good enough. But I also adore being here in Surrey. I love competing, but it's so nice to come home."

PICTURE CREDITS

GETTY: 5, 11, 12, 15, 16, 18, 19, 30, 31, 32, 33, 34, 35, 38, 44

PRESS ASSOCIATION: 4, 5, 12, 13, 14, 17, 28, 29, 30, 32, 36, 37

ANDY NEWBOLD: 2, 3, 8, 43, 47

KIT HOUGHTON: 6, 9, 20, 21, 41

ANDREW CROWLEY: 40

First published in Great Britain in 2011
by Orion Children's Books
a division of the Orion Publishing Group Ltd
Orion House
5 Upper St Martin's Lane
London WC2H 9EA
An Hachette UK Company

1 3 5 7 9 8 6 4 2

Text copyright © Orion Children's Books 2011

The right of Orion Children's Books to be
identified as the author and illustrator of this work
has been asserted.

Text written and compiled by Sally Byford.

All rights reserved. No part of this publication
may be reproduced,
stored in a retrieval system, or transmitted, in any
form or by any means,
electronic, mechanical, photocopying, recording
or otherwise, without
the prior permission of Orion Children's Books.

The Orion Publishing Group's policy is to
use papers that are natural, renewable and
recyclable products and made from wood
grown in sustainable forests. The logging and
manufacturing processes are expected to conform
to the environmental regulations of the country
of origin.

A catalogue record for this book is available from
the British Library.

ISBN 978 1 4440 0266 9

Printed in Spain by Cayfosa-Quebecor

www.orionbooks.co.uk